ESL

ADDISON-WESLEY

E

ACTIVITY BOOK

Michael Walker

Addison-Wesley Publishing Company

Reading, Massachusetts • Menlo Park, California • New York • Don Mills, Ontario
Wokingham, England • Amsterdam • Bonn • Sydney • Singapore • Tokyo • Madrid • San Juan

Contents

Featuring READING SKILLS: Understanding sequence in conversation 4, 17, 30, 43, 56, 69 ◆ Comprehension questions 11, 23, 24, 37, 38, 50, 51, 63, 64, 67, 76, 77 ◆ Word search puzzles 10, 36, 49, 59, 62, 75 ◆ Making inferences 57, 69, 77 ◆ Developing awareness of language 13, 38, 78 ◆ Reading for details 15, 24, 37, 50, 63, 76 ◆◆ WRITING SKILLS: Guided/Creative writing 13, 14, 26, 27, 39, 40, 52, 65, 66, 79 ◆ Relating personal experiences/ideas 14, 39, 40, 78, 79 ◆ Writing a poem/using poetic language 39, 52, 65 ◆◆ STUDY SKILLS: Using the dictionary 7, 20, 33, 46, 59, 72 ◆ Alphabetizing 7, 20, 46 ◆ Research report 53 ◆ Interpreting/Completing a chart 3, 43, 80 ◆ Interpreting a map 28, 72 ◆◆ PREPARATION FOR STANDARDIZED TESTING: 15, 28, 41, 54, 67, 80 ◆◆ LINGUISTIC SKILLS: Habitual present 5, 8, 57 ◆ Grammar in context 5, 9, 21, 31, 45, 57, 71, 73 ◆ Simple past (regular) 5, 9, 47, 48 ◆ Simple past (irregular) 21, 34, 47, 48 ◆ Describing future actions 17, 18, 19 ◆ Passive voice 47, 48 ◆ Present perfect 35 ◆ Distinguishing verb and noun forms 55, 68 ◆ *Some, any* 44, 45 ◆ Prepositions 57 ◆ Prefixes and suffixes 61 ◆ Using adjectives and adverbs 60, 61, 64, 70, 71 ◆ Singular and plural possessives 31, 73 ◆ Pronunciation 8, 33

A Publication of the World Language Division

Contributing Writer: Robert Saitz

Editor-in-Chief: Judith Bittinger

Project Director: Elinor Chamas

Editorial Development: Judith Bittinger, Peggy T. Alper

Production/Manufacturing: James W. Gibbons

Design, Art Direction, and Production: Taurins Design Associates, New York

Cover Art: Paul Goble

Illustrators: Mena Dolobowsky 4, 16, 17, 29, 30, 31, 44, 63; Eldon Doty 71, 74; Susan Lexa 7, 15, 41; Karen Schmidt 11, 37, 50, 51, 76; Nina Wallace 3, 72

ISBN 0-201-57823-9

3 4 5 6 7 8 9 10-WC-95 94 93 92

Sports Day

The boys and girls from Skunk, Rocky City, and Fish schools are
having a sports day. They are competing in several events. Below
is the scoreboard. The winner of each event gets four points. The
team in second place gets two points. The team in third place
gets one point (for effort!).

Event	Skunk	Rocky	Fish
Relay race	4	2	1
High jump	1	4	2
50-yard dash	1	2	4
Long jump	2	4	1
3-legged race	4	1	2

*Look at the chart below. Fill in the missing information about
the teams in the school competition.*

	First	Second	Third
Relay race	Skunk	Rocky	Fish
High jump	Rocky	Fish	Skunk
50-yard dash	Fish	Rocky	Skunk
Long jump	Rocky	Skunk	Fish
3-legged race	Skunk	Fish	Rocky

(After Level E, student pages 4-5.) **Identifying people, places, and actions; interpreting/completing a chart.**
Students will enjoy filling in the chart. They can compare answers and discuss school competitions. Ask them
how many points each team earned and which teams won the most events.

A. Circle the letter of the best response.

1. Have you seen my sweater anywhere?
   - (a.) No, I haven't.
   - b. No, I don't.
   - c. No, I didn't.

2. Where did you leave it?
   - a. A few minutes ago.
   - (b.) In the kitchen.
   - c. Last night, I think.

3. My glasses are missing.
   - a. There you go.
   - b. Here it is.
   - (c.) Here they are.

B. Complete the conversation.

I can't find my sweater.   _Where did you put sweater_ ?

~~This morning, I think.~~   _____ .

I've already looked there.   _I found it._ .

Good idea . . . here it is!

C. Match the sentences with the pictures.

1. Have you seen my book?   _D_
2. My kitten is missing.   _A_
3. I left it on the bus.   _F_
4. Try under the bed.   _C_
5. You'd better report it.   _B_
6. It's in the closet.   _E_

(After Level E, student pages 6–7.) **Understanding sequence in conversations; describing location; matching pictures with written language.** After students complete exercises independently, they can role-play Exercises A and B for dialogue practice. In Exercise C, on lines provided, students write letters of pictures that correspond with numbered sentences.

4

A. *Make questions, as in the example.*

Example: *Why don't you go to town?*

Because I don't want to go to town.

1. *Why don't you go river and swim* ?

Because we don't like to swim in the river.

2. *Why doesn't she watch the TV* ?

Because she doesn't want to watch TV.

3. *Why they are not playing tennis* ?

Because they don't like to play tennis.

4. *Why he is not going home* ?

Because he doesn't want to go home.

B. *Make sentences, as in the example.*

Example: Mike took a taxi to town. (bus)

Why didn't he take a bus ?
Because he wanted to take a taxi .

1. Judy made tea. (coffee)

Why didn't Judy made coffee ?
Because she wanted to make tea .

2. Bob bought a dog. (cat)

Why didn't Bob bought a cat ?
Because he wanted to buy a dog .

3. Inez left yesterday. (today)

Why didn't Inez left today ?
Because she wanted to left yesterday .
leave

4. Paolo sent a letter. (card)

Why didn't Paolo sent a card ?
Because he wanted to send a letter .

(After Level E, student pages 8-9). **Habitual present; simple past; short answers; grammar in context.** Students complete Exercises A-D on pages 5 and 6 independently; correct in class. Exercises A and B can be used for dialogue practice.

C. *Answer these questions about the story on student page 9.*

1. How does Hector usually behave at school?

   _____

2. Why did Hector get ten dollars?

   _____

3. Why couldn't Hector answer the teacher's questions?

   _____

4. Why did Hector want the teacher to call on Betty?

   _____

5. Why did Hector want the bell to ring?

   _____

D. *Choose words from this list to complete the sentences.*

questions	teacher	dollars	homework	thinking	study
fool around	ring	spend	whisper	night	

Hector usually doesn't _____ in school. Some students may

_____ but Hector doesn't. He does his _____ and

listens to the _____ .

Last _____ Hector got ten _____ for his

birthday. Now he is _____ of how to _____ his

ten dollars. But the teacher is asking _____ about the

homework and Hector is worried because he didn't _____ last

night. The teacher is looking at Hector and he is waiting for the bell to

_____ .

(After Level E, student pages 8-9). **Habitual present; simple past; short answers; grammar in context.** Students complete Exercises A-D on pages 5 and 6 independently; correct in class. Exercises A and B can be used for dialogue practice.

A B C D E F G H I J K L M N O P Q R S T U V W X Y Z

A. *Put these words into alphabetical order. Look at the first letter of each word.*

dragon   mouse   chipmunk   alligator   zebra

1. _____   2. _____   3. _____   4. _____   5. _____

B. *Put these words into alphabetical order. Look at the first and second letters of each word.*

cream   country   clock   children   cake

1. _____   2. _____   3. _____   4. _____   5. _____

C. *Which word or phrase is not in the right alphabetical order?* _____

firefighter   mayor   bus driver   police officer   schoolteacher

D. *Help them stand in line.*   *Write the order.*

bus driver   _____

painter   _____

shopkeeper   _____

mayor   _____

artist   _____

judge   _____

police officer   _____

disc jockey   _____

salesperson   _____

dancer   _____

firefighter   _____

(After Level E, student pages 10–11.) **Using the dictionary.** These exercises review alphabetizing (introduced in Level D). Remind students to look at the first and second letters of each word in Exercise D. Students may check each other's work.

7

A. *Mark the correct sound.*

	t	d	id
1. The dog jump**ed** into the lake.	X	___	___
2. The show start**ed** at 9.	___	___	___
3. They play**ed** tennis.	___	___	___
4. She want**ed** an egg.	___	___	___
5. He stopp**ed** at 8.	___	___	___
6. The horse pull**ed** the cart.	___	___	___
7. Nothing happen**ed**.	___	___	___
8. She wait**ed** for me.	___	___	___
9. He paint**ed** a cat.	___	___	___

B. *Make questions, as in the example.*

Example: _What did they play_ ?

They played tennis.

1. _____ ?

She likes cats.

2. _____ ?

They leave at six.

3. _____ ?

We stopped at four o'clock.

4. _____ ?

He opens the windows every morning.

5. _____ ?

I asked my teacher.

6. _____ ?

She helped her mother.

(After Level E, student pages 12–13.) **Choosing the right verb form; describing present, habitual, and past actions; spelling; grammar in context.** Do Exercise A, page 8, orally with whole class. For Exercise B, page 8, remind students to use verb in sentence, not *do*, and to be careful with tenses. Exercise C, page 9, can be "sports interview" role-play; students can check each other's work in Exercise D, page 9.

8

C. *Answer the questions about the story on student page 13. Use co[r]*
   sentences.

1. Who reported the soccer news?

   _____

2. What teams played yesterday?

   _____

3. Who scored early for the Bobcats?

   _____

4. Who looked good for the Rockets?

   _____

5. How did the game end?

   _____

6. What did the fans do?

   _____

   _____

D. *Tell the story. Use the words in parentheses and write*
   sentences on the lines below.

1. What did they want?   (bikes)
2. Where did they look?   (newspaper)
3. Which number did they call?   (617 555 2132)
4. Who answered?   (nobody)
5. When did they try again?   (7 p.m.)
6. Who answered?   (boy)
7. How much did he ask for the bikes?   ($50.00)
8. When did they pick them up?   (the next day)

1. _____   5. _____

2. _____   6. _____

3. _____   7. _____

4. _____   8. _____

(After Level E, student pages 12–13.) **Choosing the right verb form; describing present, habitual, and past actions; spelling; grammar in context.** Do Exercise A, page 8, orally with whole class. For Exercise B, page 8, remind students to use verb in sentence, not *do*, and to be careful with tenses. Exercise C, page 9, can be "sports interview" role-play; students can check each other's work in Exercise D, page 9.

9

How many food words can you find? First, write the missing
letters to complete the words. Then find and circle the words in
the puzzle.

BR E A D   CAR R O T S   SA N D W I C H
J E L LY   YEL L O W   BUT T E R
P E A N U T   S O U P   P I Z ZA
TO M A TO   CH I C K EN   M I L K
AP P L E S   J U ICE   P E A R
L E TT U C E   O R A N GES   E G G
J AM   R ICE   B A N AN A S
S A L A D   CH E ESE   F I S H

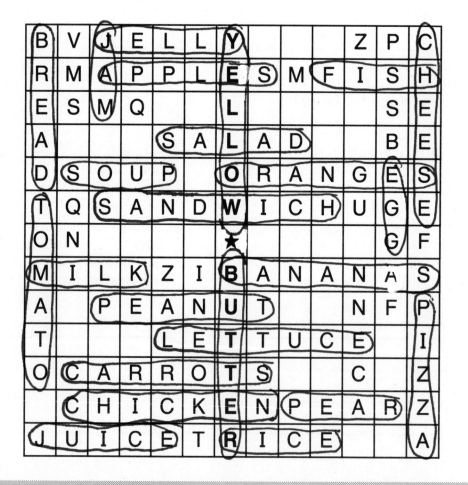

(After Level E, student page 17.) **Solving a puzzle; vocabulary development.** Students can do word-search
puzzle independently or in pairs.

Read the article and answer the questions.

Captain James Cook, the English explorer, sailed in the Pacific Ocean. In 1770, he explored the east coast of what is now Australia. He asked the natives about the strangest animal he had ever seen. The natives said, "Kangaroo!" That means, more or less, "It would be hopeless to try to tell you."

Kangaroos still fascinate us today. They are members of the marsupial family. That means they are mammals with pouches. Do you remember the marsupial you learned about in the last book?

Well, like koalas, kangaroos are vegetarians. They don't eat other animals. And like koalas, their babies are tiny when they are born. A newborn kangaroo is less than one inch long! It finds its way to its mother's pouch and lives there for many months.

Kangaroos love to box. A kangaroo's hands are very much like a human's hand. A kangaroo "puts its fists up," holding them close to its chest. Then it jabs and hops and punches, just like a prize fighter.

1. What continent did Captain Cook explore in 1770?

   Australia

2. What family of animals does the kangaroo belong to?

   Members of marsupial family.

3. What is special about marsupials?

   They are mammals with pouches.

4. How big is a newborn kangaroo?

   less than one inch long

5. Where does a baby kangaroo live during the first months of its life?

   Finds its way to its mother's pouch

6. Why does a kangaroo sometimes look like a prize fighter?

   Because jabs and hopes and punches.

(After Level E, student page 18.) **Comprehension questions.** The reading passage is identical to the listening exercise just completed on student book page 18. Accept long or short answers. Students can role-play answers in "kangaroo-expert interview" and in the process correct their own work.

11

A Man, His Son, and a Donkey

A. *Looking at the story in your book, put these events into the correct sequence (order). The first one and the last one are already numbered for you.*

_____ The man and his son met a farmer.

_10_ The man said, "In the end, you please nobody . . . not even yourself."

_____ The man and his son met an old woman.

_____ The boy climbed on the donkey's back.

_1_ The man's wife said, "sell the donkey."

_____ The boy climbed off the donkey and the man climbed on.

_____ Both the man and his son rode on the donkey.

_____ The donkey ran away.

_____ They tied the donkey to a pole.

_____ The man and his son started to walk to town.

B. *True or False? Put a* **T** *on the line after the sentence if the sentence is true. Put an* **F** *on the line if the sentence is false. Rewrite the false sentences to make them true.*

1. The man, his wife, and his son were very rich. _____

_____

2. The first person to ride on the donkey was the boy. _____

_____

3. It was an old man who suggested that both the boy and his father ride on the donkey. _____

_____

4. A farmer suggested that they carry the donkey to town. _____

_____

(After Level E, student pages 20–23.) **Putting events in a story in sequence; determining true/false statements; rewriting.** Students may work alone or in pairs. Correct in class.

A Man, His Son, and a Donkey

After the donkey ran away, what happened? Fill in the blanks with words from the choices below to complete the story. Use other words if you like them better.

The donkey _____ very fast away from the town. Soon he came to
a _____ . He felt tired, so he decided to have a _____ .
When he woke up, he saw a dragon standing _____ him! "I hope you
are a _____ dragon," the donkey said.

"Oh, my yes," the dragon _____ . "It's very lonely here. I could use
a friend."

"Well, I'm hungry," said the donkey. Do you have _____ to eat?"

"Oh, my yes, I do. Would you like some dragon _____ ? Or perhaps
some dragon _____ ?"

"I'll have some of both, please," said the donkey. The donkey followed the
dragon to the dragon's _____ . The dragon built a fire. He breathed
in, then out, and _____ came out of his _____ ! When
the food was ready, the two friends _____ it very much.

1. raced ran	2. forest mountain	3. nap rest	4. in front of beside	5. friendly nice
6. said answered	7. anything something	8. stew soup	9. pie snacks	10. cave castle
11. fire flames	12. nose mouth	13. enjoyed liked		

(After Level E, student pages 20–23.) **Guided/creative writing; developing sensitivity to language; enjoying literature.** After they complete stories independently, students can compare word choices and then role-play the parts of narrator, donkey, and dragon.

13

A Man, His Son, and a Donkey

At the end of the story, the man says to his son, "You can't please everybody. In the end, you please nobody . . . not even yourself." Think of some experiences you have had that may be examples of what the man meant. Explain what happened and why they are examples of not being able to please everybody, "not even yourself."

Write your ideas here.

_____

_____

_____

_____

_____

_____

_____

_____

_____

_____

_____

_____

_____

_____

_____

_____

(After Level E, student pages 20–23.) **Creative writing; analyzing meaning in literature; relating personal experiences.** Discuss the "moral" of the story thoroughly before assigning writing task. Some students may be more comfortable working with partners or in small groups. Volunteers can share their work with the class.

Read the story and answer the questions. Fill in the oval of the correct answer.

Neroli Fairhall is an archer from New Zealand. An archer is someone who shoots arrows at a target. But Neroli is a special archer because she cannot stand; she has to sit in a wheelchair.

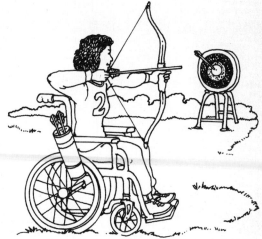

Neroli was in the 1984 Olympics in Los Angeles, California. She was the first person who was unable to walk who was in the Olympics. Many people were surprised that she could compete from a wheelchair. But she said, "For archery, it doesn't matter if you can't use your legs. Your arrows have to hit the target."

When Neroli was 24 years old, she fell off her motorcycle on a road in New Zealand. She spent seven long months in the hospital. She couldn't move her legs, and she had to learn to live all over again.

Archery was a part of Neroli's recovery. She couldn't move her legs, but she could move her arms. Neroli's first try at archery was not very successful, but soon her arrows were hitting the middle of the target, the bull's eye. She won four Australian championships, and then she won a gold medal in the 1982 Commonwealth Games.

1. Why were people surprised to see Neroli in Olympic competition?
   ◯ She was from New Zealand.
   ◯ She lost the use of her legs in a motorcycle accident.
   ◯ Archers depend mostly on the use of their legs.

2. Why did Neroli become an archer?
   ◯ Archery is the national sport of New Zealand.
   ◯ She was naturally talented with the bow and arrow.
   ◯ Archery helped her to recover from her accident.

3. Where did Neroli win a gold medal?
   ◯ At the 1982 Commonwealth Games
   ◯ At the 1984 Los Angeles Olympics
   ◯ At the 1983 Australian Championships

(After Level E, Unit 1.) **Preparation for standardized testing.** You may choose to go over unfamiliar vocabulary before giving test; or you may prefer to allow students to experience encountering new material in a test situation. Remind the students to read the directions carefully before beginning and to darken ovals completely.

15

Look at the pictures and answer the questions below.

1. Why did the cat climb the tree?

_____

2. Why did someone call the fire department?

_____

3. Why couldn't the firefighter get the cat?

_____

4. How did the cat get down?

_____

5. Where did the cat fall?

_____

6. How did the firefighters get the cat out?

_____

7. Where did they take the cat?

_____

8. What did the vet discover the next morning?

_____

(After Level E, student pages 24–25.) **Identifying people, places, and actions; vocabulary development.**
Accept long or short answers, but encourage students to use pronouns and past tense verbs. Students can
correct by role-playing newspaper reporters interviewing "witnesses."

A. *Circle the letter of the best response.*

1. How many shows are there?
   a. On Monday.
   b. In the evening.
   c. Three a day.

2. Which show shall we go to?
   a. Let's get tickets.
   b. The one in the evening.
   c. The tickets are cheaper.

3. How much is it?
   a. Five dollars each.
   b. At 7:30.
   c. Only for children.

4. What time does it start?
   a. Three dollars each.
   b. Yes, it does.
   c. At 7:30.

B. *Imagine that you are going to attend the events described on the posters. Tell where you are going, when you are going, and how much it costs.*

Example:

Dolphin Show

Afternoon 2–4 p.m.
Evening 6–8 p.m.
Adults $10.00
Children $ 6.00

I'm going to see the Dolphin Show in the afternoon. It starts at 2 p.m., and it costs six dollars for me and ten dollars for my dad.

1.

CIRCUS

Saturday, May 7
1:00 p.m.
Adults $8.00
Children $4.00

2.

General Cinema
"The Plants That Eat Plants"

Evening shows:
6–8 p.m. 9–11 p.m.
Adults $5.00
Children under 14 $3.00

(After Level E, student pages 26–27.) **Understanding sequence in conversations; describing planned future actions.** Students can do Exercise A as dialogue practice and share their answers to Exercise B.

17

A. *Make questions using* **going to**.

Example: *Where are you going to study* ? In the library.

1. _____ At eight o'clock.

2. _____ To buy some bananas.

3. _____ She's going by plane.

4. _____ Ten dollars.

5. _____ In the park.

B. *Tell what you think was going to happen.*

Example: John was on his way to the post office.

He was going to mail a letter.

1. Anita was on her way to the grocery store.

_____

2. The Browns were on their way to a restaurant.

_____

3. Lili was on her way to the library.

_____

4. Ali was on his way to the swimming pool.

_____

5. Michael was on his way to the bank.

_____

6. Tina was on her way to the movies.

_____

7. Louis and Abbey were on their way to the airport.

_____

(After Level E, student pages 28–29.) **Describing past and future actions using going to; reviewing Wh-words.** Students can work independently; correct in class. Exercise A, page 18, can be used for dialogue practice. Accept "Ali was going to swim" or "Ali was going to go swimming" for number 4, Exercise B, page 18.

18

C. *Make sentences, as in the example.*

Example: (Jonathan) writing/writer

Jonathan is interested in writing.
He's going to be a writer.

1. (Hannah) painting/painter

_____

_____

2. (Paula) acting/actress

_____

_____

3. (David) nursing/nurse

_____

_____

4. (Arnold) sailing/sailor

_____

_____

5. (Julie) dancing/dancer

_____

_____

6. (Erica) farming/farmer

_____

_____

7. (Dan) flying/pilot

_____

_____

(After Level E, student pages 28–29.) **Describing past and future actions using going to; reviewing Wh-words.** Students can work independently; correct in class. Exercise A, page 18, can be used for dialogue practice. Accept "Ali was going to swim" or "Ali was going to go swimming" for number 4, Exercise B, page 18.

19

A. *Put the days of the week into alphabetical order.*

_____ _____ _____ _____

_____ _____ _____

B. *Now put the months of the year into alphabetical order.*

_____ _____ _____ _____

_____ _____ _____ _____

_____ _____ _____ _____

C. *Here are the names of some oceans and seas. Put them into alphabetical order.*

Arctic Ocean   Atlantic Ocean   _____   _____
Indian Ocean   Pacific Ocean
Black Sea   Red Sea   _____   _____
North Sea   Caribbean Sea

                                _____   _____

                                  _____   _____

D. *These are the names of some rivers. Put them into alphabetical order.*

Mississippi   Volga   _____   _____
Amazon   Missouri
Nile   Zambesi   _____   _____
Thames   Yukon

                                  _____   _____

                                  _____   _____

E. *Now look at the names of some lakes. Put them into alphabetical order.*

Victoria   Huron   _____   _____
Ontario   Superior
Erie   Michigan   _____   _____

                                  _____   _____

Try to find the places in Excercises C, D, and E in an atlas!

(After Level E, student pages 30–31.) **Using the dictionary; more alphabetizing practice.** Have the students write the days of the week and the months of the year on a separate piece of paper to help them to do Exercises A and B. As a class, you can use an atlas to locate places in Exercises C, D, and E.

A. *Complete the paragraph by writing the correct form of the verbs in parentheses.*

By four o'clock in the afternoon, the wind (begin) _began_

to blow very hard. Harry (throw) _threw_ his ball

into the air and it quickly (fly) _~~flought~~_ over the _flown_

fence. He (go) _went_ into his house and asked his

mother, "(Do) _Did_ you (see) _saw_

the weather report on TV?" She answered, "No, I

(be) _being_ asleep and I (do, see) _don't see_

anything."

B. *Fill in the blanks with the correct form of the verb.*

1. ~~knows~~
   ~~knew~~
   ~~has known~~

   Asako _knows_ a lot about first aid. She

   knew about it for a long time because her

   father is a doctor. That's why she _has known_ what

   to do when her friend cut herself.

2. ~~have flown~~
   ~~fly~~
   flew

   Most airline pilots are very experienced. They _have flown_

   for thousands of miles before they go to work for an airline.

   Some of them also _fly_ their own small

   planes when they are not working.

3. ~~come~~
   ~~comes~~
   ~~came~~

   My father usually _come_ home from work

   about 6:00 P.M. But last night he _Comes_

   home at 4:00. He said, "I've _Came_ home

   early, so we can eat supper now and go out to a movie."

(After Level E, student pages 32–33.) **Describing past actions using irregular simple past and past participles; grammar in context.** Students work independently; correct in class. They may need help with Exercise D, page 22.

21

C. *Answer the questions about the story on student page 33.*
   Use complete sentences and past perfect forms of the verbs.

   Example: Why was the writer happy after two weeks?

   She was happy because tiny leaves had come up.

   1. Why did they move to a new house?

   _____

   2. Why was the fence on the ground?

   _____

   3. Why was the yard dirty?

   _____

   4. Why did the writer want to grow something, too?

   _____

D. *Complete these sentences, using the past perfect or the*
   simple past. Be careful!

   Example: (fly/plane/Los Angeles) because he had done it before

   He flew the plane to Los Angeles because he had
   done it before.

   1. (fly/at night) because she had worked all day

   _____

   2. She didn't want to visit the statue because (be/there/last year)

   _____

   3. They didn't want to stay all evening because (come/afternoon)

   _____

   4. (eat/at the party) because they had eaten at home

   _____

   5. (see/movie) because they had seen it before

   _____

(After Level E, student pages 32–33.) **Describing past actions using irregular simple past and past participles; grammar in context.** Students work independently; correct in class. They may need help with Exercise D, page 22.

How many animal names can you find? First, write in the letters to complete the animal names. Then find the names and circle them in the puzzle.

ALL I GATOR   R ABBIT   GOR I LL A

B E AR   R O O STER   H I PP O P O T A M U S

CA M EL   S E AL   HO R SE

D EER   SH A RK   KANGAR O O

D O G   SN A K E   LI O N

D O NK E Y   TIG E R   M O NK E Y

E A GL E   T U RTLE   M O USE

ELEP H ANT   WH A LE   P A NDA

FO X   ZEB R A   P O L A R B E AR

GI R AFF E

Animals I Know

K	D	X	H	I	P	P	O	P	O	T	A	M	U	S
A	O	M	O	N	K	E	Y	O	N	F	O	X	T	N
N	G	B	T	C	A	M	E	L	F	Z	E	B	R	A
G	D	E	E	R	D	F	H	A	J	V	R	T	C	K
A	L	L	I	G	A	T	O	R	X	H	O	R	S	E
R	M	E	D	L	I	O	N	B	N	R	S	E	A	L
O	G	P	A	N	D	A	G	E	A	G	L	E	X	G
O	O	H	B	T	H	N	C	A	P	I	B	T	K	D
V	R	A	K	T	I	G	E	R	M	R	C	J	M	O
B	I	N	W	R	J	H	X	S	H	A	R	K	O	N
E	L	T	U	R	T	L	E	T	M	F	P	V	U	K
A	L	M	R	O	O	S	T	E	R	F	K	N	S	E
R	A	B	B	I	T	W	H	A	L	E	P	L	E	Y

(After Level E, student page 37.) **Solving a puzzle; vocabulary development.** Students can do word-search puzzle independently or in pairs.

23

Read the story and answer the questions.

Ishmael had no job and no money. He left home and got a job as a sailor on a whaling ship. The Captain of the ship was named Ahab. Most of his men thought he was crazy. Ahab had only one leg. A great white whale had bitten off the other leg. All Ahab wanted to do was find that whale and kill it. He called the whale Moby Dick.

Ahab and his crew sailed across the Pacific Ocean. They reached the island of Java. A few days later, they found Moby Dick.

1. Why did Ishmael become a sailor on a whaling ship?

_____

2. What did the crew think of Captain Ahab?

_____

3. How did Captain Ahab lose his leg?

_____

4. What did Ahab want to do to the whale he was looking for?

_____

5. What name did Ahab give the whale?

_____

6. What ocean did Ahab and his crew sail across?

_____

7. What island did they sail to?

_____

8. When did they find Moby Dick?

_____

(After Level E, student page 38.) **Comprehension questions.** Accept long or short answers. The reading passage is identical to the listening exercise just completed on student book page 38. Students can exchange papers to correct.

To Count the Stars

Circle the letter in front of the correct answer.

1. One of the reasons Annie Cannon loved the stars was that
   - a. she lived on a farm.
   - b. her mother loved them.
   - c. her sister loved them.
   - d. she saw them from her roof.

2. When Annie was growing up, girls were not expected to be interested in
   - a. agriculture.
   - b. mathematics.
   - c. science.
   - d. reading.

3. Annie went to college in the state of
   - a. Delaware.
   - b. California.
   - c. New York.
   - d. Massachusetts.

4. Annie began her job at Harvard in
   - a. 1893.
   - b. 1895.
   - c. 1894.
   - d. 1892.

5. Spectrograms are
   - a. photographs of the stars.
   - b. photographs of the moon.
   - b. photographs of the planets.
   - d. photographs of the sun.

6. Spectrograms show that no two stars
   - a. make the same spectrum band.
   - b. can be photographed by the same telescope.
   - c. have the same temperature.
   - d. move at the same rate.

7. Annie arranged the stars into classes according to their
   - a. size.
   - b. distance from the earth.
   - c. temperature.
   - d. rate of travel.

8. Annie's record book of the stars made her
   - a. jealous.
   - b. curious.
   - c. serious.
   - d. famous.

9. Annie said that she was successful because
   - a. she was patient.
   - b. she was lucky.
   - c. she was a genius.
   - d. she was heroic.

(After Level E, student pages 40–43.) **Multiple choice completion; comprehension questions.** Correct in class after students do individually. They may find question number 6 tricky (the answer is *a*).

25

To Count the Stars

Pretend you are on a journey in outer space. Fill in the blanks with words from the choices below to complete your diary. You can use other words, too.

I blasted off in the year _____ . My ship is called

_____ . I have _____ crew members and _____
  2   3   4

_____ on board. We have traveled _____ miles so far. We
  5   6

are searching for a star that broke away from its orbit around _____ .
                                                                 7

The star is called _____ . The star was colonized in 2135, but we
                     8

don't know if the people there are still alive.

Today, my pilot _____ thought she heard a signal from the star.
                   9

We are on a _____ course and traveling at _____ miles
              10   11

per hour. The signal is getting _____ . We must find the star soon,
                                  12

but we can't go beyond the planet _____ . Its people are at war with
                                     13

the people of _____ . The area is too dangerous to fly through. I'll
                14

know by _____ if we have to turn back.
          15

1. 2344 2225	2. Enterprise 16 Moonbeam 1	3. ninety three	4. ten fifty	5. astronomers scientists
6. 2,000,000 5,500,000	7. Zircon Ram	8. Specto Orion 8	9. Max Tess	10. westerly northern
11. 80,000 150,000	12. stronger weaker	13. Tron Igort	14. Hugo Zeeb	tomorrow tonight

(After Level E, student pages 40–43.) **Guided/creative writing.** After filling in the blanks, the students can compare word choices and read each other's stories.

To Count the Stars

Continue the diary of your space trip. Did you find the star? Where? Were the people alive? Who did you meet? How did you help them? If you didn't find the star, what happened next? (Perhaps you were attacked. Perhaps you got lost. Perhaps you were hit by a meteor.)

Use your imagination and write your diary entries here.

_____

_____

_____

_____

_____

_____

_____

_____

_____

_____

_____

_____

_____

_____

_____

_____

_____

(After Level E, student pages 40–43.) **Creative writing.** Brainstorm the writing-prompt questions before assigning writing task. Some students may be more comfortable working with partners or in small groups. You may wish to teach the students diary format, with dates (in the future!) for this exercise. Volunteers can share their work with the class.

Look at the map and answer the questions. Circle the letter of the correct answer.

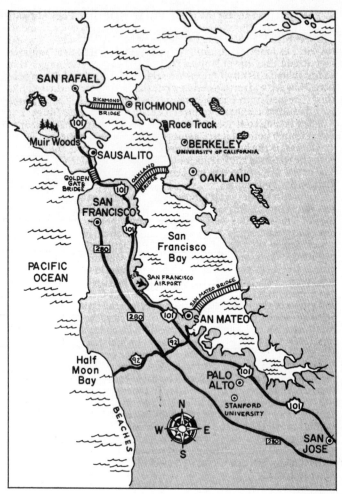

1. The highway that goes from San Francisco to San Jose is _____ .
   A. 101
   B. 92
   C. 280

2. Route 101 goes _____ .
   A. north and south
   B. east and west
   C. neither A nor B

3. Stanford University is _____ of the University of California at Berkeley.
   A. east
   B. south
   C. north

4. San Francisco Airport is beside _____ .
   A. Half Moon Bay
   B. The Pacific Ocean
   C. San Francisco Bay

5. _____ is the bridge to cross to get from San Francisco to Muir Woods.
   A. San Mateo Bridge
   B. Golden Gate Bridge
   C. Richmond Bridge

6. Palo Alto is closest to Route _____ .
   A. 101
   B. 92
   C. 280

(After Level E, Unit 2.) **Preparation for standardized testing.** Remind students to read instructions carefully. Advise them to look at the map very carefully to discern answer to number 1 (answer: 101).

A. *Choose words from the list and write them in the correct balloons.*

~~wing~~   ~~tail~~   ~~engine~~   ~~control tower~~
~~baggage~~   ~~runway~~   ~~mechanic~~   ~~cockpit~~

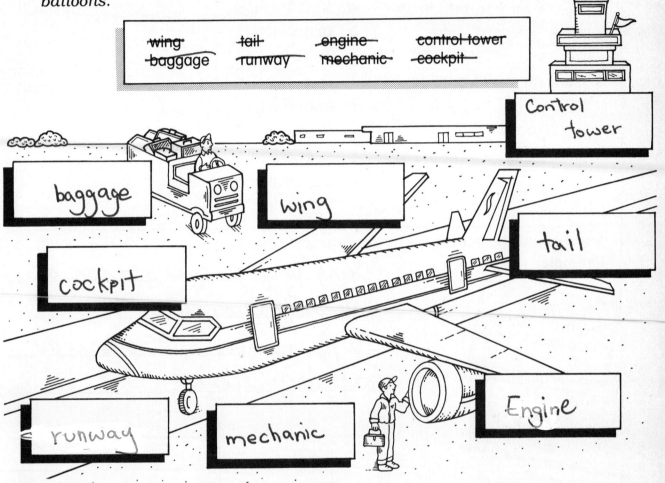

Control tower

baggage

wing

tail

cockpit

runway

mechanic

Engine

B. *Match the words with their meanings.*

1. crew   __E__
2. takeoff   __f__
3. baggage   __h__
4. seat belts   __g__
5. passengers   __c__
6. snacks   __d__
7. meteorologist   __b__
8. cockpit   __a__

a. the place where the pilot sits in an airplane
b. the people who are taking a trip on a plane, bus, etc.
c. someone who studies the weather
d. light meals, usually eaten quickly
e. the people who work on a plane, ship, etc.
f. a movement in which a plane leaves the ground and rises
g. belts attached to a seat, worn for safety
h. the bags and suitcases that are used to carry things when people travel

(After Level E, student pages 44–45.) **Vocabulary development.** For Exercise B, have the students write letter of appropriate definition of each word on lines provided. They can check each other's work after completing exercises independently.

29

A. *Circle the letter of the best response.*

1. Where do you want to go?
   a. Next Tuesday.
   b. By train.
   c. To Hawaii.

2. How do you want to go?
   a. One way.
   b. Round trip.
   c. By plane.

3. When do you want to go?
   a. Next month.
   b. Supersaver.
   c. By balloon.

B. *Write about the tickets, as in the example.*

Example: (Josef)

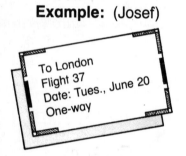

To London
Flight 37
Date: Tues., June 20
One-way

Josef is flying to London on Tuesday, June 20, on Sun Air flight number 37. He has a one-way ticket.

1. (Susana and Carmen)

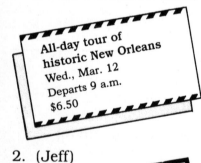

All-day tour of
historic New Orleans
Wed., Mar. 12
Departs 9 a.m.
$6.50

2. (Jeff)

Express from Baltimore
to New York City
Friday, Nov. 25
$45.00
Round-trip

(After Level E, student pages 46–47.) **Understanding sequence in conversations; using travel vocabulary.**
Exercise A can be used for dialogue practice. Students may need help with Exercise B.

A. *Choose from* **me, my,** *or* **mine,** *and fill in the blanks.*

1. This TV belongs to _____ . It's _____ .

2. That bike belongs to _____ , too. It's _____ bike.

3. _____ sister always gets letters, but no one writes to _____ .

B. *Choose from* **you, your,** *or* **yours,** *and fill in the blanks.*

1. _____ glasses are in my room. Don't _____ need them?

2. If this is my textbook, where is _____ ?

3. _____ camera is beautiful. _____ should take good care of it.

4. My notebook looks terrible, but I like _____ .

C. *Choose from* **them, their,** *or* **theirs,** *and fill in the blanks.*

1. I've lost my glasses. Have you seen _____ ?

2. This is our car, but it looks exactly like _____ .

3. Look at _____ . They're wearing _____ new soccer uniforms.

4. The Gallonis have found _____ dog, but the Swansons haven't found _____ yet.

D. *Answer the questions, as in the example.*

Example: What's Tim looking for?

He's looking for his glasses.

1. What's Jenny looking for?

_____

2. What's Mustafa looking for?

_____

3. What's Rita looking for?

_____

(After Level E, student pages 48–49.) **Possessive adjectives and pronouns; object pronouns; grammar in context.** Students complete exercises individually; correct as a class, or have students correct each other's work. For Exercise E, page 32, accept long or short answers and help students with reported speech (numbers 7–10).

E. *Answer these questions about the story on student page 49.*

1. Where were Joan and Stan going?

   They were going to San Francisco.

2. How were they traveling?

   _____

3. Why were they in a hurry?

   _____

4. Where did they want to meet their friends?

   _____

5. Why did Joan turn off on a side road?

   _____

6. What happened when Joan turned off the road?

   _____

7. Who was sitting by the side of the road?

   _____

8. What did Joan ask the farmer at first?

   _____

9. What did the farmer say about the airport?

   _____

10. What did he say about the highway?

    _____

11. What did the farmer say at the end of the conversation?

    _____

12. Who do you think felt foolish, the farmer or Joan?

    _____

(After Level E, student pages 48–49.) **Possessive adjectives and pronouns; object pronouns; grammar in context.** Students complete exercises individually; correct as a class, or have students correct each other's work. For Exercise E, page 32, accept long or short answers and help students with reported speech (numbers 7–10).

32

A. *Circle the letter in front of the best answer.*

1. An iceberg is very dangerous for ships because

   a. it has nine parts.   b. most of it is under the water.

   c. most of it is above the water.

2. An inventor is a person who has made

   a. an inventor.   b. an invent.   c. an invention.

3. An airplane pilot who used the jet stream would travel faster in

   a. the winter.   b. the summer.   c. the autumn.

4. Abraham Lincoln was president of the United States

   a. in the Middle Ages.   b. in 1860.   c. in 1920.

5. If there is a fire in your house and you want to climb down from your bedroom window, you can use a

   a. launch.   b. leaf.   c. ladder.

6. If you want to take a trip, you can go in a

   a. jay.   b. jeep.   c. knight.

7. A lake is larger than a

   a. pond.   b. sea.   c. ocean.

B. *Sometimes we don't pronounce all the letters in an English word. For example, we don't pronounce the last letter of the word autum**n**.*

1. Look at the alphabet list on page 51 of your student book. Write the three words on that page whose first letters are not pronounced.

   _____   _____   _____

2. Which letter in the word *lamb* is not pronounced?   _____

3. Which letter in the word *walk* is not pronounced?   _____

4. Which letter in the word *sign* is not pronounced?   _____

5. Look at the words *write* and *right*. In which of   _____
   them is the first letter not pronounced?

(After Level E, student pages 50–51.) **Using the dictionary; vocabulary development; pronunciation rules.**
Students refer to the Study Skills section in the student book (pages 50–51) to do Exercise A and parts of
Exercise B.

33

A. *Choose verbs from the list and fill in the blanks with their correct forms.*

| buy | read | sit | sing | cost | write | go |

1. She can't _____ a new jacket because it

   _____ too much.

2. I like a song when the singers _____ about their feelings.

3. When we _____ to my grandparents' house, we usually _____ and talk with them.

4. On the first day of class, the teachers _____ their names on the chalkboard.

5. Henry gets good grades in English because he _____ for an hour every night.

B. *Fill in the blanks with the correct form of the verbs in parentheses.*

1. Yesterday I felt sick. I think I (eat) _____ something bad. My

   mother (say) _____ , "Stay in bed." She (give) _____

   me a glass of pink stuff and I (drink) _____ it all. I felt better.

   Then I (read) _____ a magazine. At five I (get) _____

   hungry and my mother (bring) _____ me some crackers.

2. Tommy was running through the room, and he (hit) _____

   Lisa's birdhouse and (break) _____ it. He felt bad, so he (build)

   _____ another one. First, he (draw) _____ a picture.

   Then he (find) _____ some wood. He (build) _____

   the house and (cut) _____ a hole for the birds to get in.

   Then he (buy) _____ a little flag for the house. The flag

   (cost) _____ a dollar but Tommy was happy.

(After Level E, student pages 52–53.) **Irregular verbs; simple past/past participles; present perfect.** Students complete exercises independently; they may need some help with Exercise D, which can be used for dialogue practice. Review verbs from previous levels or units (*go, eat, give, get,* etc.).

C. *Cross out the word that is not correct.*

Example: John ~~run~~/ran two miles yesterday.

1. She hit/hitted her head against the door.

2. They have wrote/written three letters this morning.

3. That dress cost/costed eighteen dollars.

4. She has took/taken that test before.

5. We have cutted/cut that tree four times already.

6. He had spoken/spoke to his father before Mr. Lyons called.

7. She sung/sang at the chorus last night.

8. Lisa sweeped/swept the floor because there was glass on it.

9. Then my father brought/brang the dessert.

D. *Write sentences, using the correct verb forms.*

Example: you/see/alligator   *Have you ever seen an alligator?*

see/raccoon/last week   *No, but I saw a raccoon last week.*

1. you/run/two miles _____

   run/mile/last year _____

2. she/sit/in a movie/4 hours _____

   sit/in a concert/3 hours/once _____

3. you/buy/superduper sundae _____

   buy/banana split/yesterday _____

4. he/bite/a person _____

   bite/another dog/last week _____

5. they/find/money/in the park _____

   find/a dollar/in the street/last night _____

(After Level E, student pages 52–53.) **Irregular verbs; simple past/past participles; present perfect.** Students complete exercises independently; they may need some help with Exercise D, which can be used for dialogue practice. Review verbs from previous levels or units (*go, eat, give, get,* etc.).

35

How many "feelings" words can you find? First write the missing letters to complete the words. Then find and circle the words in the puzzle.

M __ D
FRI __ __ __ LY
EX __ __ __ ED
__ __ RAI __
LO __ __ LY
__ __ RT

EM __ __ __ RAS __ __ D
P __ __ __ D
G __ __ D
HA __ __ Y
__ __ GRY
WOR __ __ __ __

__ __ __ EPY
S __ __ K
__ HY
S __ __ __ ED
K __ N __
__ __ D

E	C	L		E	R	G	L	A	D		P	M
M	A	D	C	X		T	S	I	C	K	X	J
B	M	R		C		E		S	W	S	H	Y
A		D		I	A	**F**	R	A	I	D	A	B
R		F		T	**E**		D			P	E	
R		R		E	**E**		T	G	H	P	F	
A		I		D	G	**L**	O	N	E	L	Y	V
S	L	E	E	P	Y	**I**		F	I	Q	W	K
S	A	N		L	**N**		D		H		I	
E		D		A	N	**G**	R	Y		U		N
D		L		C	**S**	S	C	A	R	E	D	
P		Y		B		U	N		T		Z	
P	R	O	U	D	O	W	O	R	R	I	E	D

(After Level E, student page 57.) **Solving a puzzle; vocabulary development.** Students can solve word-search puzzle individually or in pairs. Some students may circle *feelings*.

Read the article and answer the questions.

Elephants live in Africa and in India. The African elephant is bigger than the Indian elephant. But they are both big! They are so big that they rarely lie down. They even sleep standing up. It's just too much trouble, getting more than eight thousand pounds up and down.

The elephant's trunk is very sensitive. It can pick up a single piece of grass. Its trunk is also very strong. It can lift more than two thousand pounds—more than a ton. The elephant's trunk has many uses. The elephant uses it to eat, drink, breathe, communicate, and smell with.

The life span of the elephant is similar to that of humans. It lives about seventy years. It is among the most intelligent of wild animals and is almost unbeatable in a fight.

1. Where do elephants live?

_____

2. Why do elephants sleep standing up?

_____

3. What is special about an elephant's trunk?

_____

4. What does an elephant do with its trunk?

_____

5. How long does an elephant usually live?

_____

6. What helps an elephant live a long life?

_____

(After Level E, student page 58.) **Comprehension questions.** Accept long or short answers. The reading passage is identical to the listening exercise just completed on student book page 58. Students can role-play interview with "elephant expert" to check their answers.

Tom Paints the Fence

A. *Answer the questions about the story.*

1. Why did Tom think his friends would make fun of him?

   _____

2. Why did Tom pretend not to notice Ben at first?

   _____

3. How did Tom get Ben interested in whitewashing the fence?

   _____

4. What did Ben offer Tom for the "privilege" of whitewashing?

   _____

5. Why did the other boys come to watch Tom whitewash the fence?

   _____

6. What did each boy have to do to get a turn whitewashing?

   _____

7. Why did Tom finally have to stop the whitewashing "party"?

   _____

8. Who did most of the work, Tom or his friends?

   _____

B. *Tom Sawyer* was written in the nineteenth century. Some of the language is old fashioned. Rewrite these sentences, using more modern language. Which style do you think is more interesting?

   Example: Ben ranged up alongside Tom.   *Ben slowly moved closer to Tom.*

   1. "You're up a stump, aren't you?"   _____

   2. "Say, I'm going in a-swimming. . . ."   _____

   3. "No, no, I reckon not."   _____

(After Level E, student pages 60–63.) **Comprehension questions; developing awareness of language style.** Accept long or short answers for Exercise A. Students may need help with Exercise B. Correct and discuss both exercises in class.

Tom Paints the Fence

A. *Fill in the blanks with words from the choices below, or use other words to complete the poem.*

_____ Tom Sawyer, one of the boys,
     1

_____ his _____ and got
   2   3

Their toys.

They came to _____ and have some fun,
           4

But Tom _____ them,
       5

_____ .
   6

The boys all _____ to take Tom's place,
        7

_____ Tom just hid the smile on
   8

His face.

1. Young
   Smart
	2. Tricked
	   Fooled
		3. friends
		   pals
			4. jeer
			   laugh

5. outdid
   outsmarted
	6. Every one
	   One by one
		7. begged
		   asked
			8. While
			   And

B. The boys gave Tom their favorite things. If you had been there, what would you have traded? Tell about one of your favorite things. Was it a present? Did you buy it yourself? Why do you like it?

_____

_____

_____

_____

_____

(After Level E, student pages 60–63.) **Guided/creative writing.** Students can compare word choices for Exercise A and volunteers can share their answers to Exercise B. (Point out convention of capitalizing the first word in each line of a poem.)

39

Tom Paints the Fence

Think about the last line of the story:

> In order to make a man or a boy covet a thing, it is only necessary to make the thing difficult to attain.

Is there something you want very, very much? Why do you want it? Is it difficult to get? How are you trying to reach your goal of getting it? How do you think you will feel if you reach your goal? How will you feel if you don't reach your goal?

Write your thoughts here.

_____

_____

_____

_____

_____

_____

_____

_____

_____

_____

_____

_____

_____

_____

_____

_____

(After Level E, student pages 60–63.) **Creative writing.** Depending on the level of your group, go over writing-prompt questions *or* have students attempt assignment without preliminary discussion. But be sure the students understand the words *covet* and *attain*. Volunteers can share their essays.

Circle the letter of the sentence that means the same as the underlined sentence.

1. Joan and Stan were on their way to San Francisco.
   A. They were traveling toward San Francisco.
   B. They were leaving San Francisco.
   C. They needed a way to get to San Francisco.

2. Joan and Stan were going by car.
   A. They were going to buy a car.
   B. They weren't going in a car.
   C. They were going in a car.

3. They were in a hurry.
   A. They were on an empty highway.
   B. They wanted to go quickly.
   C. They wanted to go slowly.

4. Joan turned off on a side road.
   A. Joan couldn't find the side road.
   B. Joan drove the car from the highway to a side road.
   C. Joan turned the car over on a side road.

5. How can we get back to the highway?
   A. How can we turn off the highway?
   B. How can we turn around on the highway?
   C. How can we return to the highway?

6. Joan was getting impatient.
   A. Joan didn't want to wait any longer.
   B. Joan was becoming ill.
   C. Joan was becoming tired.

7. There was a lot of traffic on the highway.
   A. There were a lot of cars on the highway.
   B. There were police officers on the highway.
   C. There was an accident on the highway.

(After Level E, Unit 3.) **Preparation for standardized testing.** Remind students to follow test directions carefully. (Test is follow-up to page 49 of student book.)

41

A. *What are they called? Fill in the blanks with the name of the worker.*

1. A _____ is someone who works in a restaurant and brings food to the tables.

2. A _____ is someone who works in a bakery and bakes bread and pastry.

3. A _____ is someone who writes scripts for actors.

4. A _____ is someone who operates a camera for a movie or a TV show.

B. *Complete the sentences below, using the correct forms from this list.*

reader-reads	driver-drives	designer-designs	director-directs
writer-writes	producer-produces	actor-acts	

1. The _____ reads from a script that tells him what to say.

2. A director _____ everybody. She explains where to stand or move.

3. The _____ of a show is the one who is in charge of everybody else.

4. Kevin _____ poems, and he would like to be a

   _____ when he is older.

5. There are many kinds of designers. A set designer on a TV show

   _____ sets, while a dress _____ designs dresses.

6. People who cannot see often get a _____ who

   _____ books to them.

7. You're not supposed to talk to the _____ when he

   _____ the bus.

(After Level E, student pages 64–65.) **Describing people, actions, and occupations; vocabulary development.**
Students may need to be reminded of vocabulary for Exercise A (*waiter, baker*, etc.). Students can exchange papers to correct both exercises.

A. *Circle the letter of the best response.*

1. Can I take your order?
   a. To the kitchen.
   b. Yes, thanks.
   c. My order.

2. Something to drink?
   a. Chocolate ice cream.
   b. Tuna sandwich.
   c. Some milk.

3. Anything for dessert?
   a. Chicken pie.
   b. Cheese pizza.
   c. Carrot cake.

B. *Look at the menu.*

MENU			
Soups	**Sandwiches**	**Beverages**	**Desserts**
Chicken $1.00	Tuna $2.50	Coffee $.50	Ice cream $.75
Tomato 1.25	Egg 2.25	Tea .50	Fresh fruit .75
	Ham 2.25	Milk .75	Carrot cake .75

Frank, Maria, and Lucy are in the restaurant. Frank has $6.50.
Maria has $5.75. Lucy has $7.30. Frank does not want soup.
Maria does not want dessert. Lucy wants soup and dessert. They
all want sandwiches and beverages. What can they buy?

Fill in the chart.

	Frank	Lucy	Maria
Soup			
Sandwich			
Beverage			
Dessert			
What is the total cost?			

(After Level E, student pages 66–67.) **Understanding sequence in conversations; reading a menu and making food/money choices; simple math.** Exercises A and B can be combined into a restaurant role play; the students may need to use scratch paper to add up menu prices.

A. *Look at the picture and answer the questions.*

Examples: Is there any milk? (juice)

No, there isn't any milk, but there is some juice.

Are there any knives? (forks)

No, there aren't any knives, but there are some forks.

1. Is there any butter? (cheese)

_____

2. Is there any salt? (pepper)

_____

3. Is there any bread? (crackers)

_____

4. Are there any apples? (oranges)

_____

5. Are there any soup spoons? (teaspoons)

_____

6. Are there any saucers? (cups)

_____

(After Level E, student pages 68-69.) **Describing quantity (count/non-count; some/any); grammar in context.**
Exercises A and B can be used for dialogue practice. Note that Exercise A, number 3 (page 44) requires use of
singular and plural in the same sentence. Instruct students to use *some* and *any* or *something* and *anything* in
their answers to Exercise C (page 45).

B. *Complete the conversation. Use* **some** *and* **any.**

Waiter: Hi, would you like _____ juice?

Kim: Yes, thanks. I'd like _____ orange juice.

Waiter: I'm sorry. We don't have _____ orange

juice, but we have _____ apple juice.

Kim: O.K. I'll have _____ apple juice. Do you

have _____ sandwiches today?

Waiter: No, there aren't _____ sandwiches today,

but there is _____ turkey soup.

Kim: O.K. I'll have _____ turkey soup, please.

C. *Answer the questions about the story on student page 69.*
Use complete sentences.

1. Why did Frank go shopping?

_____

2. What did he see in the first store?

_____

3. Why did he leave the first store?

_____

4. What did he see in the second store?

_____

5. What kind of yarn did he buy?

_____

6. Why did he want to buy the yarn?

_____

7. Why didn't Frank want to bring his dog in to be measured?

_____

(After Level E, student pages 68-69.) **Describing quantity (count/non-count; some/any); grammar in context.**
Exercises A and B can be used for dialogue practice. Note that Exercise A, number 3 (page 44) requires use of
singular and plural in the same sentence. Instruct students to use *some* and *any* or *something* and *anything* in
their answers to Exercise C (page 45).

45

A. *Fill in the blanks with the correct answers.*

1. If you are in the army or navy, you have to _____ an officer.

   a. orbit   b. charge   c. obey   d. decide

2. A piece of iron may be attracted to a _____ .

   a. measure   b. pond   c. steel   d. magnet

3. The Nile is one of the longest _____ in the world.

   a. ponds   b. lakes   c. rivers   d. oceans

4. You can use a needle to _____ something.

   a. cook   b. sew   c. obey   d. measure

5. A planet may move in _____ .

   a. a nest   b. an orbit   c. a code   d. a pole

6. The Step Pyramid was built in Egypt _____ the Olympic Games in Greece.

   a. before   b. after   c. at the same time as

7. A polar bear is a _____ animal.

   a. small   b. pet   c. red   d. large

B. This is an alphabet code:

A B C D E F G H I J K L M N O P Q R S T U V W X Y Z

Z Y X W V U T S R Q P O N M L K J I H G F E D C B A

Use the code and fill in the correct words below.

If you are walking in the SRNZOZBZH _____ ,

you probably will see a lot of HMLD _____ . You may

also see an VZTOV _____ or a

ULC _____ , but you probably don't have to be

ZUIZRW _____ of seeing an VOVKSZMG

_____ or an ZOORTZGLI _____ . I'm

pretty sure you'll never see a WIZTLM _____ .

Choose a word that you like and write it in the code. _____

(After Level E, student pages 70–71.) **Using the dictionary; vocabulary development; alphabet code.**
Students refer to Study Skills section in student book (pages 70–71) for Exercise A (they may need help with number 6). Students will enjoy "cracking" alphabet code (Exercise B). Check answers in class.

46

A. *Complete the sentences, using the correct form of these verbs:*

buy	find	break	sing	build	bring	drive

Example: The car __was__ __driven__ into the car wash by my father.

1. That yarn _____ _____ by a man with a dog.

2. That song _____ _____ by the Menudo.

3. My house _____ _____ by my father and his brothers.

4. The dessert _____ _____ by another waiter.

5. Those cups _____ _____ by a large dog.

6. The spoons _____ _____ in the top drawer.

B. *Match these phrases and write the sentences below.*

1. The Step Pyramid was built   are held every four years.
2. A newspaper is published   by Imhotep.
3. The thread is put   by a magnet.
4. Olympic prizes were given   to the best athletes.
5. The Morse Code   every day or once a week.
6. The modern Olympics   was invented by Samuel Morse.
7. Iron is attracted   through a hole in the needle.

1. _____

2. _____

3. _____

4. _____

5. _____

6. _____

7. _____

(After Level E, student pages 72–73.) **Using verbs in passive voice.** In Exercise A, remind students to switch from *was* to *were* for numbers 5 and 6. You may want to do Exercise D (page 48) with the class, as it is quite difficult. Give the students a hint: don't use the adjective when the sentences are combined.

C. *Fill in the blanks with the passive form of the verbs in parentheses.*

The Egyptian pyramids (build) _____ about 4500 years ago.

They (use) _____ to bury the Egyptian kings. The body of a king

(put) _____ inside and then the pyramid (shut) _____ .

The pyramids (make) _____ without machines. First, big

stones (cut) _____ into blocks. Some of them (bring) _____

from far away. The blocks (take) _____ to the pyramid. There

they (push) _____ and pulled until the workers had built a high

pyramid. Then the pyramid (cover) _____ with white stones.

D. *Write sentences as in the example.*

Example: That machine is excellent. Electricity runs it.

That machine is run by electricity.

1. These video games are fun. All the kids play them.

   _____

2. Those robots are amazing. A computer controls them.

   _____

3. These shoes are very comfortable. An athlete designs them.

   _____

4. That TV show is good. Ming produces it.

   _____

5. These floors are clean. The fifth graders sweep them.

   _____

(After Level E, student pages 72–73.) **Using verbs in passive voice.** In Exercise A, page 47, remind students to switch from *was* to *were* for numbers 5 and 6. You may want to do Exercise D with the class, as it is quite difficult. Give the students a hint: don't use the adjectives when the sentences are combined.

How many verbs can you find? First, write the missing letters to complete the words. Then find and circle the verbs in the puzzle.

F __ __ D	ST __ __ Y	__ __ SS	__ ALK
DR __ __ E	__ __ LL	SL __ __ E	S __ __ P
__ __ IMB	DR __ __ K	J __ __ P	GR __ __
WO __ __	S __ __ M	R __ W	P __ __ H
__ __ ILD	__ OG	R __ N	__ __ ATE
ST __ __ T	S __ __ G	C __ __ W __	O __ __ N
__ AN __ __	E __ T	LIS __ __ __	DI __ __
__ SK	S __ I	RI __ __	F __ __ L
W __ __ K			

M	D	S	C	R	A	**W**	L	P	N	O	S	R
F	A	L	L	V	E	**A**	T	B	S	P	I	O
I	N	I	I	Z	M	**L**	I	S	T	E	N	W
N	C	D	M	X	S	**K**	I	P	U	N	G	X
D	E	E	B	D	M		C	D	D	Y	P	O
P		Q	T	R	J	**O**	G	I	Y		U	
M	I	S	S	I	D	**R**	I	V	E	A	S	K
X			N	Z			E			H		
B	W	O	R	K	X	**S**	K	I		R	U	N
U				C	**T**	A	L	K	G	B	S	
I		P	U	L	L	**R**	I	D	E	R		W
L				J	**U**	M	P		O			I
D			S	K	A	**T**	E			W		M

(After Level E, student page 77.) **Solving a puzzle; vocabulary development; verb review.** Students can solve word-search puzzle individually or in pairs. Unfamiliar word: *strut.*

49

Read the story and answer the questions.

I'll never forget the day that Billy Bones came to live in our Inn. He was tall and strong, and his black pigtail hung on his shoulders. He had a white scar across one cheek. Billy Bones had sailed on the pirate ship of Captain Flint. He told me that he had Flint's map—the map that showed where Flint had buried all his pirate treasure. Billy was very afraid of just one man. "If you ever see a one-legged sailor come in here, warn me!" he said. He paid me a penny to be on the watch.

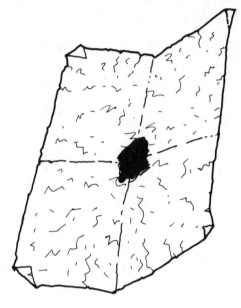

One day, a blind seaman came to see Billy. He put something in Billy's hand. "The Black Spot!" Billy cried in fear. "Jim Hawkins, listen. This means my old shipmates are coming to get me! They're after my map, boy."

And with that, Billy Bones fell dead at my feet.

1. What was Billy Bones like?

_____

2. Who was Captain Flint?

_____

3. What was on Captain Flint's map?

_____

4. Who was Billy Bones afraid of?

_____

5. Why did Billy Bones give Jim Hawkins a penny?

_____

6. Who came to see Billy one day?

_____

7. What did Billy's old shipmates want from him?

_____

(After Level E, student page 78.) **Comprehension questions.** Accept long or short answers. The reading passage is identical to the listening exercise just completed on student page 78. Correct in class.

The Blue Lake

Fill in the blanks to complete these sentences.

1. The Taos Indians have lived in New Mexico for over _____ years.

2. The Spanish word for *village* is _____ .

3. The Taos Indians' houses are made of *adobe*, which consists of

   _____ .

4. The Taos Indians raise _____ , _____ , and _____ .

5. Water for the village comes from the _____ .

6. In _____ , the government took the Taos Indians' _____

   and the _____ away from them.

7. In 1926, the government offered the Taos Indians _____ if they
   would give up their claim.

8. The bill passed by the Senate of the United States returned to the

   Taos Indians _____ and _____ .

9. The fight had lasted for _____ years.

10. For the Taos Indians, selling their land is like selling the

    _____ .

(After Level E, student pages 80–83.) **Comprehension questions; experimenting with color.** As a follow-up
bring in pictures of turquoise stones or jewelry. Have students experiment with blues, greens, and yellows to
make turquoise. If possible, use water colors.

51

The Blue Lake

Here are some short poems to complete, using words from the choices below. Notice that they don't rhyme, so you can choose any words that appeal to you. After you have completed the poems, write one of your own. Perhaps you will write about the moon or the sun. Perhaps you'll choose to describe a lake or a forest or a river.

1.
The mountain is _____ ;
                       1
It wears a _____ of _____ ,
             2   3
And a _____ of pine trees.
         4

1.	beautiful	2.	cap
	lovely		crown
3.	clouds	4.	robe
	snow		dress

2.
The ocean _____ like a _____
             1   2
When winter _____ blow,
            3
_____ the waves into the _____
    4   5
_____ sky.
   6

1.	roars	2.	lion
	moves		tiger
3.	storms	4.	Lifting
	winds		Whipping
5.	cold	6.	Gray
	icy		Dark

3.
Stars _____ in a _____
       1   2
sky,
Like _____ on an umbrella
      3
Raised above the _____ .
              4

1.	shine	2.	cloudless
	twinkle		black
3.	diamonds	4.	world
	jewels		earth

_____

_____

_____

_____

_____

_____

(After Level E, student pages 80–83.) **Guided/creative writing.** Before students attempt their own poetry writing, discuss imagery (metaphors, similes, personification) with class, pointing out examples in poems here (and/or elsewhere). Encourage students to include imagery in their poems.

52

The Blue Lake

Use reference books to find some more information about Pueblo Indians. What state besides New Mexico do they live in? About how many Pueblo Indians are there in the Southwest? What do they do besides raise animals? What is their diet like? Where do the children go to school? What else did you learn about Pueblo Indians?

Write your report here. Use extra paper if you need more space.

_____

_____

_____

_____

_____

_____

_____

_____

_____

_____

_____

_____

_____

_____

_____

_____

_____

(After Level E, student pages 80–83.) **Research report.** Take the class to the school or other library or provide encyclopedias and other reference materials for this assignment. Students will need help researching and organizing their reports. You may wish to make this pair or small-group work. Volunteers can report their findings to the class.

Find the spelling mistakes in these stories. Fill in the ovals next to lines that contain spelling mistakes. If a story does not have any spelling mistakes in it, fill in the oval next to "No mistakes."

Example:

- ⬤ The first Olympic gams took place in 776 B.C. The lasted for
- ⬤ three days. At the end of three days, prises were given to the
- ◯ best performers. Then there was a great feast, or dinner.
- ◯ (No mistakes)

1. ◯ Morse Code is a way to comunicate using dots and dashes for leters
   ◯ of the alphabet. Samuel Morse invented it in 1837. Dashes are
   ◯ long signalls. Dots are short signalls.
   ◯ (No mistakes)

2. ◯ A pyramid is a solid having triangular sides meeting in a point.
   ◯ The first pyramid was the Step Pyramid. It is in Egypt. The sides
   ◯ of all other pyramids are smoth.
   ◯ (No mistakes)

3. ◯ The Nile is a great river in Africa. It flows north through
   ◯ Egypt and empties into the Mediterranean Sea. Most experts
   ◯ agree: the Nile is the longest and greatest river in the world.
   ◯ (No mistakes)

4. ◯ An oficer is a person who commands others in an army or navy.
   ◯ An oficer may hold publick office or be the president, secatary,
   ◯ or treasurer of a club or company.
   ◯ (No mistakes)

5. ◯ A needle is a very small, sharp tool used for sewing. A needle
   ◯ has a sharp point at one end and an eye or whole at the other
   ◯ end to put the thread through.
   ◯ (No mistakes)

(After Level E, Unit 4.) **Preparation for standardized testing.** Remind students to follow directions carefully in a test situation. Go over example with students, and tell them that some lines may contain more than one spelling mistake.

A. Match the occupation with the phrase that describes it.

1. a secretary _____   a. prepares food in a restaurant
                          b. sells things
2. a mechanic _____   c. collects money
                          d. helps people who are sick
3. a switchboard operator _____   e. works on a radio or TV show
                          f. puts gasoline in your car
4. a salesperson _____ g. repairs engines, changes tires,
                             etc.
5. a gas station attendant _____   h. works in a office, keeps
                             records, etc.
6. a chef _____   i. works with telephones

7. a doctor _____

8. an announcer _____

9. a cashier _____

B. Here are some words that can be used as both nouns and verbs. Complete the sentences with the correct forms.

repair	record	answer	wash	change	pump	check

1. Clara Fender is the chief mechanic. She and her helpers _____ cars and trucks.

2. Ella makes sure all the gas _____ are full every morning.

3. Fred Suds can _____ a car in about two minutes at the car

   _____ .

4. At Whit Wheeler's, customers are allowed to pay their bills by _____ .

5. Ask Hildy Headset anything about Whit Wheeler's business. She has all

   the _____ .

6. One of Tony Type's jobs is to _____ the names and addresses of new customers.

7. When Sun Stock isn't too busy with spare parts, he helps the mechanics

   to _____ flat tires.

(After Level E, student pages 84–85.) **Vocabulary development; distinguishing verb and noun forms.**
Students work individually and can exchange papers to correct, or correct as a class.

55

A. *Circle the letter of the best response.*

1. Congratulations!
   - a. I am, thanks.
   - b. Thank you.
   - c. Was I really?

2. You must have worked hard.
   - a. That was a lucky catch.
   - b. I *did* work hard.
   - c. Was I really?

3. You were great.
   - a. Was I really?
   - b. Well done.
   - c. Thanks, I am.

4. Your project must have taken weeks.
   - a. It really took months.
   - b. That's nice to hear.
   - c. Thanks a million.

B. *Complete the conversation.*

Congratulations! _____ .

You must have worked hard. _____ .

You should be proud of yourself. _____ .

You certainly deserved it. _____ .

C. *Now complete this conversation.*

Marie: You were the _____ player in the game today. You

were _____ .

Ann: _____ I really? I got only one _____ .

Marie: But it was a _____ hit. It was a home run, and that's why

your team _____ the game.

Ann: I think I was very _____ . I didn't think the ball was going to
go that far.

(After Level E, student pages 86–87.) **Understanding sequence in conversations; vocabulary development.**
You can use all three of the exercises on this page for dialogue practice and role plays.

A. *Use the verbs and pronouns on this list and make up sentences that describe what probably happened.*

wash	watch	myself	ourselves	each other
see	cut	yourself	yourselves	
hurt	love	himself/herself/itself	themselves	
drive	burn			

Example: My mother was cooking supper and she touched a hot frying pan.

She probably burned herself.

1. The mechanic was working on an automobile engine and his hands and face were dirty.

2. The dog ran into the living room and looked at the mirror.

3. I was putting a picture on the wall with a hammer and a nail, but the hammer hit my finger.

4. My uncle bought a saw but he didn't know how to use it. One day I saw him with a bandage on his leg.

5. Ellen and Frank decided to get married.

6. My grandfather wanted to go to the grocery store but there was nobody to drive him there. So he got into the car.

7. We wanted to see some pictures that our parents took of us when we were at the picnic. We got the movie projector and the film.

(After Level E, student pages 88–89.) **Describing habitual action; reflexive pronouns; prepositions; making inferences; grammar in context.** For Exercise A, number 4, students may need help with the past tense of *shoot.* Be sure students use *by (one)self* correctly in Exercises B and C (page 58).

B. *Complete the sentences, as in the example.*

Example: I made the sandwiches, but I (cut) *cut myself* _____.

1. Lori and I went to the concert last night. We (enjoy) _____.

2. He didn't see any friends in the movie, so he (sat) _____.

3. When I put on new clothes, I (like) _____.

4. She was going to fall off the chair, but she (stop) _____.

5. You'll probably decide to change your hat after you (see) _____.

6. They were careful when they moved the furniture because they didn't want to (hurt) _____.

7. She wrote to her mother that she wanted to (live) _____.

8. Sometimes when a dog has fleas, it (bite) _____.

C. *Answer the questions about the story on student page 89. Use complete sentences.*

1. Who did Mrs. Jones live with in the country?

_____

2. What happened to her when she fell down the stairs?

_____

3. Why didn't Mrs. Jones want to go to the hospital?

_____

4. What did the doctor tell Mrs. Jones not to do?

_____

5. When did the doctor return?

_____

6. How did Mrs. Jones get in and out of her bedroom during that week?

_____

(After Level E, student pages 88–89.) **Describing habitual action; reflexive pronouns; prepositions; making inferences; grammar in context.** For Exercise A, number 4, students may need help with the past tense of *shoot.* Be sure students use *by (one)self* correctly in Exercises B and C (page 58).

A. *Answer the questions or fill in the blanks.*

1. The bees who build and repair the hive and make honey are the

   _____ bees.

2. If you put the word *quince* into the Study Skills list, you would put it

   between the words _____ and _____ .

3. Which word has four meanings? _____

4. Why is rice so important? _____

5. Where were telephones first used? _____

6. Which word is a plural noun? _____

7. One of the words that is both a noun and a verb is _____

8. How much of the earth's surface is covered by land? _____

B. *Try this puzzle.*

Across

3 a food that needs a lot of water
  when it grows
5 the wife of a king
6 a movement of the planets around
  the sun
8 the day before tomorrow

Down

1 not noisy
2 leave
3 a disk that plays music
4 There's a mouse _____ the
  kitchen
7 abbreviation for *that is*

(After Level E, student pages 90–91.) **Using the dictionary; vocabulary development; crossword puzzle.**
Students refer to Study Skills section of their textbooks (pages 90–91) to complete Exercise A. Help them with
crossword, especially with 5-down (answer: *i.e.*).

59

A. *Use one of these adjectives to complete the sentences below.*

afraid	unafraid	lucky	unlucky
pleasant	unpleasant	fair	unfair

1. Sammy was working in the spare-parts department of a gas station when two big tires fell on him. But he didn't get hurt. Sammy was

   _____ .

2. There was a terrible storm and the airplane was dropping quickly. Hildy grabbed Susan's arm but Susan was very quiet. She seemed

   _____ . "Aren't you _____ ?" asked Hildy.

   "Not today, Hildy," Susan said. "Today is my _____ day."

3. Eddie's mom said, "I know it's an _____ job to wash the floor

   and it seems _____ because you did it last week, but your brother is sick and I need help."

B. *Complete the sentences, using the* **-ness** *form of some of these adjectives.*

round	small	strange	kind	fair	quick

1. Although his _____ sometimes bothered him, he was very comfortable in small cars.

2. In most sports players need _____ .

3. Many people are now thinking of the need for _____ to animals as well as to people.

C. *Tell why, as in the example.*

Example: useless *The car was useless because a tire was missing.*

1. **homeless** _____

2. **friendless** _____

3. **harmless** _____

(After Level E, student pages 92–93.) **Prefixes and suffixes (un-, -ness, -ful, -able).** Students complete exercises individually; correct in class. (You may wish to expand on Exercise E with the class, asking students for suggestions. Also, be sure to pronounce *eatable* for students and have them repeat after you.)

D. *Complete the sentences below, using these adjectives.*

| harmful | thankful | thoughtful | playful | careful |

1. The monkeys were having a lot of fun. They were throwing banana peels at each other.

   They seemed very _____ .

2. Mary remembers everybody's birthday, and she sends cards or presents to all her friends and relatives.

   She is very _____ .

3. Our rivers and oceans are so full of dirt and chemicals that swimming in them can be very unpleasant.

   In fact, it can be _____ .

4. She took the eggs out of the box one at a time, making sure that they didn't touch each other.

   She was very _____ .

5. On Thanksgiving, we try to have a good dinner with the whole family.

   We feel especially _____ for what we have.

E. *For each word below, list something that **can** and something that **can't** be done.*

   Example: countable *You can count apples. Apples are countable.*
   You can't count sugar. Sugar is not countable.

   1. **breakable** _____
      _____

   2. **drinkable** _____
      _____

   3. **eatable** _____
      _____

(After Level E, student pages 92–93.) **Prefixes and suffixes (*un-*, *-ness*, *-ful*, *-able*).** Students complete exercises individually; correct in class. (You may wish to expand on Exercise E with the class, asking students for suggestions. Also, be sure to pronounce *eatable* for students and have them repeat after you.)

61

How many parts of the body can you find? First, write the
missing letters to complete the words. Then find and circle the
words in the puzzle.

ST __ __ __ CH   __ __ SE   E __ R   __ O __ Y

B __ __ OD   H __ __ D   __ Y __ S   F __ __ T

M __ __ TH   __ AIR   FI __ __ __ __ S   K __ __ E

__ __ M   L __ __   EL __ __ __ S   __ AC __

T __ __ __ H   __ __ UMB   __ AND

Up To My Elbows

S	T	O	M	A	C	H	G	E	A	R
X	E	B	G	T	U	E	B	H	W	V
C	E	R	X	S	F	A	F	K	H	E
N	T	W	B	C	E	D	A	T	E	Y
T	H	U	M	B	E	S	C	R	A	E
P	C	G	H	Z	T	X	E	D	L	S
E	L	V	K	N	O	M	O	U	T	H
H	A	I	R	D	V	T	B	L	H	B
N	C	B	A	A	R	M	E	S	W	N
O	W	C	K	S	A	C	G	E	N	O
B	H	A	N	D	F	L	E	G	H	S
L	B	C	E	F	H	K	O	R	T	E
O	A	L	E	X	E	L	B	O	W	S
O	B	O	D	Y	N	B	O	L	N	T
D	N	K	U	F	I	N	G	E	R	S

(After Level E, student page 97.) **Solving a puzzle; vocabulary development.** Students can review parts of the
body and solve the word-search puzzle independently or with partners.

Read the article and answer the questions.

The prairie dog is an unusual and interesting animal. It's not really a dog. It's a cousin of the squirrel. But it barks like a dog. It has yellowish-brown fur and a short tail. The prairie dog lives on the great, grassy plains of North America. Well, it really lives under the prairie in huge, underground towns.

Each home is occupied by one male, four or five females, and their children. The homes are all connected by underground tunnels and burrows. There is a sentry at the tunnel entrance of every home. The sentries sit upright, on guard, watching for an enemy. If a sentry spots an enemy, it lets out a series of short, sharp calls. Other sentries repeat the alarm throughout the town, so everyone is on guard. Enemies of the prairie dog include coyotes, bobcats, ferrets, and hawks. Man is also an enemy. Prairie dogs are hunted in states where they are considered pests. They damage crops, since they like to eat anything that is green!

1. In what way is the prairie dog like a dog?

_____

2. What is a typical prairie dog family?

_____

3. What do the sentries do?

_____

4. Why do people hunt prairie dogs?

_____

(After Level E, student page 98.) **Comprehension questions.** Accept long or short answers. The reading passage is identical to the listening exercise just completed on student book page 98.

63

The Girl Who Loved Wild Horses

A. *Answer these questions about the story. Use complete sentences.*

1. What was special about the girl's relationship with horses?

   _____

2. Why didn't the coming storm wake the girl up?

   _____

3. What did the girl do when she finally woke up?

   _____

4. Why didn't the horses stop at her command?

   _____

5. How did the girl know they were lost?

   _____

6. What was the spotted stallion like?

   _____

7. How did the girl and the horses feel about staying with the wild horses?

   _____

B. *Often, verbs in the -ing form are used as adjectives: for example,* **galloping** *horses. Write the number of the adjectives in the left-hand column in front of the nouns they describe in the right-hand column. Some adjectives may describe more than one noun.*

1. prancing   _____   horses

2. grazing   _____   hooves

3. flashing   _____   sun

4. snorting   _____   thunder

5. rumbling   _____   lightning

6. rising   _____   grounds

7. drumming   _____   stallion

(After Level E, student pages 100–105.) **Comprehension questions; matching adjectives and nouns.** After students complete Exercise B in terms of the story, have them "mix and match"; e.g., prancing *horses* (instead of *stallion*), drumming *thunder* (instead of *hooves*), etc.

The Girl Who Loved Wild Horses

*From the choices below, fill in the blanks with the words you
like best to complete the poems. Use other words if you like the
way they describe the subject of each poem better.*

1. **"Wild Horses"**

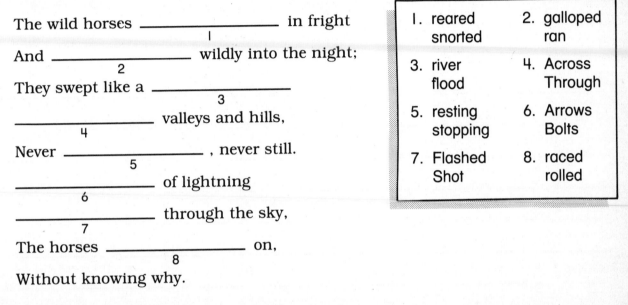

The wild horses _____ in fright

1

And _____ wildly into the night;

2

They swept like a _____

3

_____ valleys and hills,

4

Never _____ , never still.

5

_____ of lightning

6

_____ through the sky,

7

The horses _____ on,

8

Without knowing why.

1. reared snorted	2. galloped ran
3. river flood	4. Across Through
5. resting stopping	6. Arrows Bolts
7. Flashed Shot	8. raced rolled

2. **"After the Storm"**

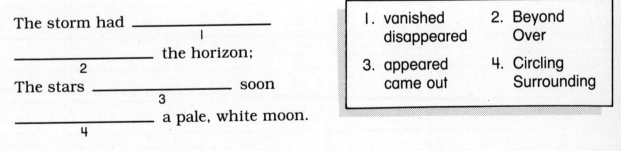

The storm had _____

1

_____ the horizon;

2

The stars _____ soon

3

_____ a pale, white moon.

4

1. vanished disappeared	2. Beyond Over
3. appeared came out	4. Circling Surrounding

3. *On a separate piece of paper, you may write a poem of
   your own about animals or the weather—or anything else.
   Try to use descriptive language.*

(After Level E, student pages 100–105.) **Guided/creative writing.** After students complete exercises 1 and 2, they can compare word choices. When they write their own poems in exercise 3, suggest they use similes and metaphors like those in "The Girl Who Loved Wild Horses." (Explain the convention of beginning the first word in each line of poetry with a capital letter.)

The Girl Who Loved Wild Horses

The beginning of the story seems quite realistic: a girl helps her mother with chores every day before going off to a meadow to be with some horses, "but. . .careful never to go beyond sight of home." But one day she not only goes far away from home, she stays away with the horses. Is this a dream the girl had when she fell asleep? Or is it a daydream—her fantasy?

Write your own ending for the story here.

_____

_____

_____

_____

_____

_____

_____

_____

_____

_____

_____

_____

_____

_____

_____

_____

(After Level E, student pages 100–105.) **Creative writing.** Brainstorm extensively before assigning writing task, which you may want to have the students do in pairs or in small groups. As a prewriting activity, have the students jot down their feelings, as well as their ideas about the story. Volunteers can read their stories to the class.

66

Read the paragraph and fill in the oval next to the correct answer.

Ever since the days of slavery, black people in the South had developed special skills in working with horses. During the first Kentucky Derby in 1875, thirteen of the fourteen riders were black. By 1882, Ike Murphy, a black man who began racing horses at the age of fourteen, had won forty-nine of fifty-one races at the Saratoga Race Track. In addition to working with horses, many black people became cowboys. Probably the most famous one was the rodeo champion Bill Pickett. Bill wrestled steers but he did not use a rope; he used his hands to make the steers lie down on their sides. This was called "bulldogging." He practiced this skill so well that he became a rodeo star and in 1971 he was admitted to the National Rodeo Hall of Fame.

1. Which would be the best title for this article?
   - "The Kentucky Derby"
   - "Bill Pickett"
   - "Blacks and Horses"

2. Which of these sentences best expresses the main idea of the paragraph?
   - Black people played an important role in horse racing and rodeos.
   - The black people who raced horses later became cowboys.
   - Black people learned to work with horses when they were slaves.

3. What is the best description of "bulldogging"?
   - A cowboy uses a rope to wrestle steers to the ground.
   - A cowboy uses his hands to wrestle steers to the ground.
   - A cowboy races a bull against a dog.

4. Which of these statements is *not* true?
   - Ike Murphy won forty-nine of fifty-one races at the Saratoga Race Track by 1882.
   - Bill Pickett was never admitted to the National Rodeo Hall of Fame.
   - Thirteen of the fourteen riders in the 1875 Kentucky Derby were black.

(After Level E, Unit 5.) **Preparation for standardized testing.** Remind students to follow directions carefully and to darken ovals completely. Subject of reading passage ties in with literature section of this unit.

67

A. *Here are some more words that can be used as both nouns and verbs. Complete the sentences with the correct forms.*

run	milk	plow	plant	water	harvest	help

1. Linda is in charge of the gas station. She _____ it with the

   _____ of her three sons.

2. Last year Terry _____ a flower garden. He _____
   the flowers every day, but it was a very dry summer and some of the flowers

   died because they didn't get enough _____ .

3. At the end of the summer when the fruits were ready, the Smiths needed

   three more workers to _____ with the _____ .

4. In the morning, Peter went out to ride the _____ over the fields

   to prepare the ground for planting, and Patty went to _____
   the cows.

_____

B. *Rewrite the sentences with the correct information.*

1. Clara feeds and milks the kitchen.

   _____

2. Lucy has six children who help her on the farm.

   _____

3. The hens lay two hundred eggs a week.

   _____

4. Peter plants the seeds before he plows.

   _____

5. Little Lucy takes care of the farm machinery.

   _____

(After Level E, student pages 106–107.) **Vocabulary development; distinguishing verb and noun forms; correcting erroneous information.** Students complete exercises individually; correct with whole group.

A. *Circle the letter of the best response.*

1. I'm sorry you lost.
   a. That would be great.
   b. So am I.
   c. Yes, I did.

2. Don't look so sad.
   a. I'll try to cheer up.
   b. I appreciate it.
   c. That would be great.

3. You'll get over it.
   a. I'm truly sorry.
   b. What a disappointment!
   c. I hope so.

B. *Complete the conversation.*

Cheer up. You tried hard. _____ .

You can always try again. _____ .

Well, better luck next time. _____ .

Come on. I'll buy you an ice cream. _____ .

C. *Underline the correct answer.*

1. She tried hard to win but her best wasn't good enough.	She probably feels	disappointed. lucky. better.
2. They cheered him up after he lost.	He probably feels	terrible. better. sorry.
3. They didn't win, but they forgot about it after they had some ice cream.	They probably	got over it. appreciated it. gave it up.
4. He tried very hard but he didn't win the prize.	He feels good because he knows that he	gave up. did his best. cheered them up.
5. They wanted to make her feel better.	They decided to	disappoint her. pity her. cheer her up.

(After Level E, student pages 108–109.) **Understanding sequence in conversations; making inferences.**
Exercises A and B can be used for dialogue practice. Instruct students to complete Exercise C by choosing
among options in third column.

69

A. *Use an adjective or an adverb form of the words on the list to answer the questions below.*

quick	fast	careful	careless
slow	kind	nervous	terrible

Example: How did Jenny speak?   *She spoke nervously.*

or

What kind of speaker is Jenny?   *She is a nervous speaker.*

1. How does Allie clean her room?   _____

2. What kind of writer is Paul?   _____

3. What kind of a worker is Pablo?   _____

4. How does Clara take care of the chickens?   _____

5. How does Laura run?   _____

6. What kind of an eater is the baby?   _____

7. How does Rashid read?   _____

8. What kind of a driver is Lucy?   _____

B. *Choose four adverbs and write four sentences describing something that you have done.*

Example: (quietly) *When I was in the library, I spoke to Ellen quietly.*

1. _____

2. _____

3. _____

4. _____

C. *Read the story on student page 111. Then fill in the blanks with the adjective or the adverb form of these words.*

proud	nervous	excited	kind	free	easy	terrible
sad	happy	hard	fast	quiet	quick	simple
loud	slow	careful	careless	patient	impatient	

Gonzalez was usually a _____ man but today he looked

_____ . He was walking _____ in front of his shop

when he heard a _____ noise. He looked around _____

because it sounded like a shot but it was only Jorge, the mechanic across the

street. Jorge was not a _____ worker; he had _____

dropped a tool, and that had made the noise. It was getting late and Gonzalez

started to walk _____ . He was _____ because Bond

had not yet arrived.

Suddenly a car came _____ around the corner. The driver was

driving _____ . It was Bond. He stopped in front of the shop and

got out. The two of them spoke _____ . Bond said, "It wasn't an

_____ job; it took me four hours but I did it. I'm _____

of my work." Gonzalez looked at Bond _____ and said, "Now I

feel good. We're safe. We can walk _____ on the streets of the city."

(After Level E, student pages 110–111.) **Using adjectives and adverbs; grammar in context.** Check exercise answers in class. For Exercise C, instruct students to read the whole story before going back to fill in the blanks. If time permits, have students read their stories to the whole class, asking their classmates to supply the answers.

71

A. *Answer the questions or fill in the blanks.*

1. Which words have the same pronunciation but different spellings?

   _____   _____

2. The word **w** __ __ __ can mean something that is inside or something that is outside.

3. Which animal described on the dictionary list is not a real animal?

   _____

4. When did the Vikings live? _____

5. __ rays can go through your body.

B. *Look at this map of the world. Put the number of the place next to its name below.*

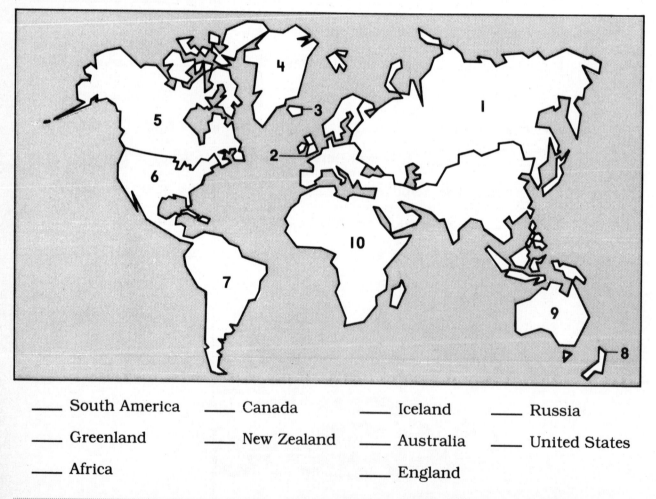

____ South America   ____ Canada   ____ Iceland   ____ Russia

____ Greenland   ____ New Zealand   ____ Australia   ____ United States

____ Africa   ____ England

(After Level E, student pages 112–113.) **Using the dictionary; vocabulary development; geography.** Students refer to Study Skills section of their student books (pages 112–113) to complete Exercise A. Do Exercise B as a class, using an atlas or the globe.

72

A. *Put the number of one of these three groups next to each sentence below.*

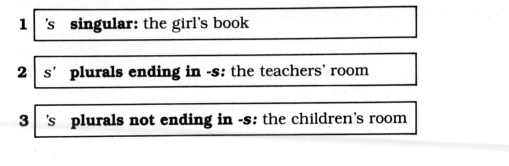

1 | *'s* **singular:** the girl's book

2 | *s'* **plurals ending in -s:** the teachers' room

3 | *'s* **plurals not ending in -s:** the children's room

Example: ___1___ Those are Peter's chickens.

1. _____ We visited the Johnsons' house.

2. _____ Don't pull the lion's tail.

3. _____ Three dentists bought an office together. The dentists' office is on Washington Street.

4. _____ They saw the women's car in the driveway.

5. _____ The children's room was painted last year.

6. _____ Where is Tran's dog?

7. _____ The cities' leaders are all in favor of the new plan.

8. _____ Harry's oldest son went to the university.

___

B. *Answer the questions, as in the example.*

Example: Whose hat is it? (John) *It's John's hat.*

1. Whose car is it? (Pat) _____

2. Whose eggs are they? (Clara) _____

3. Whose books are they? (the children) _____

4. Whose ticket is it? (Lucy) _____

5. Whose bats are they? (the men) _____

6. Whose letters are they? (the Browns) _____

(After Level E, student pages 114–115.) **Singular and plural possessives; grammar in context.** Students complete exercises independently; correct with whole class. You may wish to review the contractions *it's* and *they're* before assigning Exercise B. For exercise C (page 74), encourage use of pronouns; students should have no difficulty with reported speech (numbers 6 and 7) because examples follow text.

C. *Answer the questions about the story on student page 115.*
   Use complete sentences.

   1. What was the name of Jack's talent agency?

   _____

   2. How would you describe the Hawks' faces?

   _____

   3. Where did Mrs. Hawk's glasses sit?

   _____

   4. What kind of act was Jack Moss looking for?

   _____

   5. What kind of act did the Hawks do?

   _____

   6. Whose part did Mr. Hawk say was very exciting?

   _____

   7. What did Jack say was people's reactions to bird acts?

   _____

   8. Where did the Hawks decide to go after leaving Jack's agency?

   _____

   9. What did Mrs. Hawk do when she left Jack's office?

   _____

(After Level E, student pages 114–115.) **Singular and plural possessives; grammar in context.** Students complete exercises independently; correct with whole class. You may wish to review the contractions *it's* and *they're* before assigning Exercise B. For exercise C (page 74), encourage use of pronouns; students should have no difficulty with reported speech (numbers 6 and 7) because examples follow text.

First, write the missing letters to complete the words. Then circle the words in the puzzle that are things we find in the world or the universe.

__ __ EE	M __ __ NT __ __ NS	__ __ __ __ BOW
O __ __ __ N	__ AI __	I __ E
D __ __ ER __	PL __ __ __ TS	__ L __ __ ER __
CL __ __ D	__ __ KE __	S __ Y
S __ __ D	G __ __ SS	H __ __ L __
SE __ __ S	RI __ __ __ S	W __ __ D
__ OO __	L __ __ D	BUS __ __ __
S __ N	RO __ __ S	__ __ OW
S __ A		

S	K	Y	B	I	S	O	C	E	A	N	R	
E	M	O	U	N	T	A	I	N	S		A	
E	O		S	G	A					I	I	F
D	O		H	D	R	**O**	C	K	S	A	N	L
S	N		E	E	S	**U**	N	T	S	E	A	O
G	R	A	S	S	X	**R**	A	I	N	B	O	W
	H	S		E						E	P	E
	I	A		R				S		R	L	R
	L	N		T		**W**	I	N	D	T	A	S
	L	D	T			**O**		O		Z	N	L
	S		R			**R**	W				E	A
	I	C	E		C	**L**	O	U	D		T	N
R	I	V	E	R	S	**D**	L	A	K	E	S	D

(After Level E, student page 119.) **Solving a puzzle; vocabulary development.** Students may solve word-search puzzle individually or in pairs. Some students may circle OUR WORLD.

75

Read the story and answer the questions.

My name is Gulliver. I am a ship's doctor. My travels began on May 4, 1699. All was well for the first few weeks. Then we sailed into a storm. The ship began to sink. Six of us got into a little boat and began to row to an island. We saw the ship go down just as a huge wave upset our little boat. The five men disappeared. I swam as long as I could. Just when I knew I couldn't swim any longer, my feet touched bottom. I waded to the shore, and crawled onto the beach. There was no sign of people. I fell asleep immediately. When I woke up, I couldn't move my arms or legs. I was tied to the ground. How could this have happened? I felt something moving up my right leg. It walked up my chest and stood under my chin. I could hardly believe my eyes!

1. Why was Gulliver on the ship?

_____

2. Why did the ship begin to sink?

_____

3. How many people survived the storm with Gulliver?

_____

4. What did Gulliver see when he reached shore?

_____

5. How did Gulliver get to shore?

_____

6. What did Gulliver do as soon as he crawled onto the beach?

_____

7. What happened to Gulliver while he was sleeping?

_____

(After Level E, student page 120.) **Comprehension questions.** Reading passage is identical to listening exercise just completed on student book page 120. Accept long or short answers. Discuss the fact that answers are in the third person although the reading is in the first person. Why?

Switch on the Night

Answer the questions about the story.

1. How old do you think the little boy in the story is?

   _____

2. Why wouldn't the little boy touch a light switch?

   _____

3. Why wouldn't he play outside after dark?

   _____

4. Why was the little boy lonely and unhappy?

   _____

5. What did the little boy like instead of the night?

   _____

6. What did he do one night when his father was away and his mother was asleep?

   _____

   _____

7. Who came to the little boy's window?

   _____

8. What did Dark look like?

   _____

9. What four things did Dark and the little boy "switch on"?

   _____ _____

   _____ _____

10. At the end of the story, what did the little boy do with the other children?

    _____

    _____

(After Level E, student pages 122–127.) **Comprehension questions; making inferences based on literature.**
Have students work individually or in pairs. Accept long or short answers. Discuss students' reactions to story after correcting exercise.

77

Switch on the Night

1. "Switch on the Night" uses opposites: switch on/switch off; light/dark; happy/unhappy, etc. From the story, or from your own experience, list some more opposites.

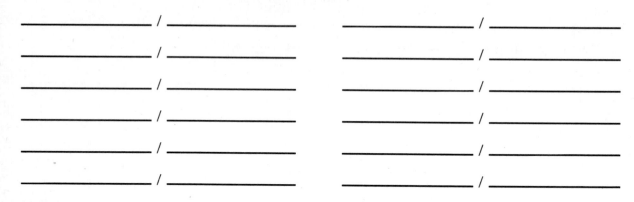

_____ / _____   _____ / _____

_____ / _____   _____ / _____

_____ / _____   _____ / _____

_____ / _____   _____ / _____

_____ / _____   _____ / _____

_____ / _____   _____ / _____

2. The story also uses repetition. For example, there is repetition of nouns (page 123): "parlor *lights*, porch *lights*," etc. There is also repetition of verbs (page 126): "*switching on* the crickets, *switching on* the frogs," etc. Find other examples of repetition in the story, or make up some similar phrases of your own.

3. What feelings are expressed in the story? What feelings did you have as you read the story? List some here.

Feelings in the story   **My feelings**

(After Level E, student pages 122–127.) **Prewriting exercises.** These activities can be done individually or in pairs. Number 3 leads directly to the creative writing activity on page 79. You may expand the exercises if appropriate for your class. Perhaps some students will be inspired to produce some poetry.

Switch on the Night

The boy in the story was afraid of the night. The girl called "Dark" helped him. Do you think she was real? Do you think the boy was dreaming? Are you sometimes afraid in the night? Who helps you when you're afraid? Do you sometimes have bad dreams? What are they about? Do you sometimes have happy dreams? What are they about? Write about a time when you were afraid or had a bad dream. Or write about a happy dream.

_____

_____

_____

_____

_____

_____

_____

_____

_____

_____

_____

_____

_____

_____

(After Level E, student pages 122–127.) **Creative writing.** Encourage students to talk over their fears, but do not insist on participation. Students have free choice to write about happy or sad feelings. Allow time for volunteers to share their work.

These charts show the average high temperatures for the different months of the year in Paris and Marseilles, two cities in France. Look at the charts and fill in the ovals next to the correct answers.

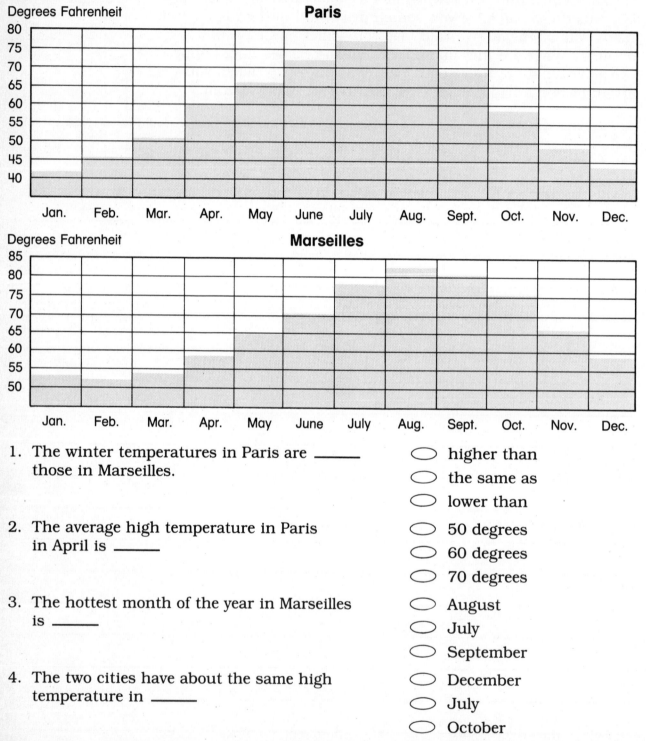

1. The winter temperatures in Paris are _____ those in Marseilles.

   ◯ higher than
   ◯ the same as
   ◯ lower than

2. The average high temperature in Paris in April is _____

   ◯ 50 degrees
   ◯ 60 degrees
   ◯ 70 degrees

3. The hottest month of the year in Marseilles is _____

   ◯ August
   ◯ July
   ◯ September

4. The two cities have about the same high temperature in _____

   ◯ December
   ◯ July
   ◯ October

(After Level E, Unit 6.) **Preparation for standardized testing.** Remind students to follow directions in tests carefully and to darken the ovals completely.